Friendship

EDITED BY ROBERT CUMMINS

ST. MARY'S COLLEGE PRESS • WINONA, MINNESOTA

PHOTO CREDITS

Paul Johnson—pages 15, 57
Jean-Claude LeJeune—pages 54, 64
Steve Murray—page 4
Norman Provost, FSC—pages, 25, 40
Ron Sievert—cover, pages 10, 11, 12, 16-17, 22-23, 29, 30-31,
    32-33, 35, 36, 50, 61, 62-63, 69, 71, 74, 77, 81, 83, 85, 88,
    91, 92-93
Vernon Sigl—pages 2-3, 7, 19, 27, 38-39, 43, 44, 49, 58, 86
Arthur C. Sturm, Jr.—pages 8, 53

First Printing—December 1971
Second Printing—June 1972
Third Printing—January 1974

ACKNOWLEDGMENTS

Selection from *Wind, Sand and Stars* by Antoine de Saint Exupery. Copyright © 1967, by Lewis Galantiere. Reprinted by permission of Harcourt Brace Jovanovich, Inc.

Selections from *The Four Loves* by C. S. Lewis. Copyright © 1960 by Helen Joy Lewis. Reprinted by permission of Harcourt Brace Jovanovich, Inc.

"The Comfort of Friends," from *The Treasure Chest,* edited by J. Donald Adams. Copyright © 1946 by E. P. Dutton and Co., Inc.

Selection from *The Art of Living* by Andre Maurois, translated by James Whitall. (Harper & Row, 1940). Reprinted by permission of Harper & Row, Publishers, Inc.

"I Like It," by Jo Thebaud. Reprinted by permission of author.

Selection from *Who Am I?* by Lowell D. Streiker, Copyright © Lowell D. Streiker, 1970, published by Sheed & Ward Inc., New York.

"Spring," by Kathleen Flynn. Reprinted by permission of author.

Selection from *Loneliness* by Clark E. Moustakas. Copyright © 1961, Prentice-Hall, Inc., Englewood Cliffs, New Jersey.

Selections from *The Ways of Friendship* by Ignace Lepp, translated by Bernard Murchland, Copyright © 1966 by The Macmillan Co.

Selection from *The Prophet* by Kahlil Gibran. Copyright © 1923 by the author. Copyright © renewed 1951 by Administrators C.T.A. of Kahlil Gibran Estate, and Mary G. Gibran. Reprinted by permission of Alfred A. Knopf, Inc.

Selection from *Of Love and Lust* by Theodor Reik. Copyright © 1941, 1944, 1957 by Theodor Reik. Copyright © 1949 by Farrar, Straus and Company.

Selection from *The Hand of a Stranger* by Jean Cocteau, Copyright © 1956 by Elek Books, Ltd. Reprinted by permission of Editions Bernard Grasset.

To those persons whom I have touched and who have touched me in friendship, especially Charlie, this book is dedicated. You are part of me and I am part of you, so this book is yours as it is mine.

TABLE OF CONTENTS

PREFACE

FRIENDSHIP is an experience all of us have enjoyed to some degree. The memory of a friendship includes gratitude for moments shared, feelings understood, anxieties lifted. And a feeling of self worth is involved—knowing that something of oneself was given and found valuable by a friend. These are the ideas presented in this book.

Perhaps it happens mainly when we are lost in our friendships or alone—away from them—that we question friendship or are critical of its meaning. We ask ourselves about the quality of our friendships, about the limitations imposed on them by culture or habit; we may begin to suspect that what we called friendship was just a near miss on love. And yet, at the same time, we believe in it so deeply. Such questions and suspicions are also brought before the reader in this book.

In most of the readings and poems here, however, the thrust is positive and hopeful. Friendship is seen as a mind-blower, a fresh wind on the spirit, a glory in life—in other words, a necessity, as C. S. Lewis writes, not in order to live, but to make living worthwhile.

PART 1

WHAT IS FRIENDSHIP?

No one can describe in words exactly what friendship is. Words are inadequate and never seem to say enough when it comes to feelings and experiences.

Friendship is sometimes the consuming joy which threatens to erupt in a scream—and sometimes it is intense pain. It is also many other things. But none of the experiences or the feelings in *themselves* are friendship. Taken together they give us some sort of a picture of friendship. But since the total experience of friendship can only be lived and felt and is not capable of being adequately described in words, the closest anyone can come is a poor description of bits and pieces of their experiences in friendship.

Friendship establishes a bond between two persons which can be broken if one wishes to break it. This ever present possibility of it being broken along with the fact that it isn't broken, is what creates the peculiar faithfulness which is typical of authentic friendships.

Those who have experienced friendship know that it is "forever." It is "forever" by its very nature and not through some extrinsic quality, even though this "being forever" depends entirely upon the free will of each friend.

2

4

The essence of friendship is entireness, a total magnanimity and trust. It must not surmise or provide for infirmity. It treats its object as a god, that it may defy both.

Ralph Waldo Emerson

The other element of friendship is tenderness. We are holden to man by every sort of tie, by blood, by pride, by fear, by hope, by lucre, by lust, by hate, by admiration, by every circumstance and badge and trifle—but we can scarce believe that so much character can subsist in another as to draw us by love.

Ralph Waldo Emerson

WHAT I MEAN BY A FRIEND

I mean something that is almost too much to be looked for in this world. I mean one whose nature is so large that it will understand and sympathize with all my myriad varied moods. I mean a man who, when he finds me mean and nasty will not despise me; when he sees me harsh and critical, will not condemn my harshness of heart; when I am cruel in judgement, or in word, or in action, will bear with me until I recover my senses; will smile and endure knowing that this is only a passing whim; when I am ill-tempered or peevish, or melancholy, will pity me and wait until the disease has run its course, and the color of health has returned.

I mean by a friend one who will give as well as take. I mean one who, when he in turn is in trouble, will not hide from me. I mean one who will not give me the everlasting feeling that the weakness is all mine, while he is in possession of unending peace and calm. I mean one who will trust me far enough to see his volume as I let him see mine, knowing that I too will not misunderstand or misinterpret or become impatient or condemn, or turn upon my heel and walk no more with him, even as I know he will not do the same to me. This is the other side of friendship harder to discover than the first. Yet if one would be my friend, in the deep sense in which I understand it, he must give me this as I give the same to him; he must trust me thus far, even as I trust him; if he is only my patron, my protector, my guide my model, my ideal, he may be very much to be loved and honored, but he is not strictly my friend.

I mean by a friend one with whom there are no differences. Whatever be our respective gifts of nature and of grace, it must be all the same between him and me. If he thinks me clever or learned, or strong or even holy, he will neither bow before me nor treat me as being of another grade; though I may know him to have rank or wealth, or athletic skill, or wit, these things, when I think of him, will scarcely enter my mind. We take each other for granted, without suspicion, without reserve, without doubt; the rest are mere appendages belonging to one as much as to the other, affecting so little our equality that we never give them a thought.

Even from the best of human friends, I can not ask more than he can give. For think of all it calls for. It calls for a mind that can understand mine without any need of words. It calls for a heart that can bleed from sympathy and fellow-feelings more than any sufferings of its own. It calls for a soul so holy, so humble in all its holiness, that it will give of its all, of its worst as well as of its best, uncovered and undisguised into the hands of its friend. It calls for a will that can go to all lengths, asking no questions, making no conditions, when the question of friendship demands it.

Anonymous

10

True friendship implies a deep trust—a belief that there is nothing in this world that is formidable enough to come between you and your friend.

Robert Brian

I do not wish to treat friendships daintily, but with roughest courage. When they are real, they are not glass threads or frostwork, but the solidest thing we know.

Ralph Waldo Emerson

13

ATTRIBUTES OF FRIENDSHIP
by Andre Maurois

Disinterestedness is a necessary attribute to real friendship and it is the duty of one friend to guess another's problems and render assistance before it is asked. If our friends have needs that we can satisfy, we should relieve them of the necessity of seeking our help.

Another essential attribute of friendship is, I believe, mutual admiration. "But," you will say, "I have friends whom I do not admire. I love them just the same, and would tell them frankly that I do not admire them." There is a confusion here and the need to probe more deeply into reality. We all have friends to whom we speak harsh truths, and indeed there can be no true friendship without this kind of sincerity. But if we can endure criticism from a friend, which, coming from another, would anger us, isn't it because we know that he admires us fundamentally?

I do not mean that he thinks we possess all the virtues or that he finds us particularly intelligent. It is more complex than that. I mean that he has carefully considered our faults and our good qualities and has chosen us; better still, he has preferred us to others.

It is very important to realize that sincerity is possible only because of this admiration. We accept any criticism from him who loves or admires us because it does not impair the self-confidence without which our life would be unbearable.

True friendship implies full confidence, which may only be completely given or completely withdrawn. If friendship has continually to be analyzed, nursed, and cured, it will cause more anguish than love itself, without having love's strength and its remedies. And if this confidence is ill-placed? Well—I would rather be betrayed by a false friend than deceive a true one.

14

15

Does absolute reliance carry with it a complete exchange of confidences? I believe that true friendship cannot exist otherwise. Jung has said that one of the objects of friendship is to reintegrate secret thoughts and feelings with ordinary social intercourse. How could a friend's admiration have any value if called forth by a fictitious *me* and not the real *me*? Until two people are able to reach down to the level of their sleeping memories, their conversation is without real interest and it languishes. But as soon as the probe goes deep enough, the spring of confidences bursts forth. Nothing is pleasanter than to be aware, during a conversation until then mechanical and boring, of this gradually increasing vividness.

Friendship, like marriage, implies a vow, which is indicated by Abel Bonnard's definition: "Friendship is the positive and unalterable choice of a person whom we have singled out for qualities that we most admire."

17

I'm doing my thing, and you're
    doing your thing.
You have no claim over me and I
    have no claim over you.
Your expectations are not barriers
    which I have to climb,
Nor should my expectations force
    you into directions you do not
    wish to go.

You are only you.
I am only myself.
But if we by chance find each other,
Then it's beautiful.

PART 2

SEARCHING FOR FRIENDSHIP

Searching presupposes that a person sees something worth searching for, that one has a reason to search. Because friendship means so much to us, because we value the relationship which friendship demands, we are always alert to people. Everyone we meet we see as a potential friend because everyone we meet has something to share with us and we feel we have something valuable to share with them.

It is important also to be constantly trying to find means of increasing and deepening the friendships in which we already share. As persons, we are constantly changing. Therefore, our relationship with our friends must also change. Friendship is not static; it is very dynamic.

A person should do two things:

Acquire a teacher
Choose a friend.

Talmud

23

We do not love our friends *despite* their human faults but simply *with* their faults because these happen to be our friends' faults and are part of him.

Friendship is like life in that we discover its nature only through experience, and this experience very quickly dissipates any romantic ideals in order to reach the deeper human values.

I NEED YOUR HELP

I want to ask you for a favor,
A big favor; it means very much to me.
I need your help to do something.

I'm trying to get to know you,
I want to be your friend.
But this is very difficult,
It is not at all easy.
Not because you are particularly hard to know,
But I am particularly poor at discovering you.

You see it is one thing to want to do something,
And another to make the effort to do it,
And still another to actually do it.

In other words, sometimes it may not seem
    like I want to be your friend.
And maybe I don't know just how to do it,
But don't let that fool you,
I'm never-the-less trying.

That's where you come in.
I'm kind of new at this,
And naturally clumsy at first,
So you've got to let me try.
You have to give me a chance.
That's why I need your help.

26

More important than that, though,
It's a two-way street,
Implying an effort from both of us.
It's a joint venture.
That is why I need your help.

I want to know you,
That's why I need your help.

Anonymous

Like the Stone of Wisdom, friendship may be lying right in your back-yard and you may never know it. Your best friend may be a stranger to you, or you may lose him because you didn't bother to hold him.

Friends must be cultivated by sincerity, frankness, and deeds of affection. No one can remain your friend if you hide your soul from him.

You needn't save face before your friend. Your friend will save it for you.

Life is a chain of little events. Close your soul to your friend and he will lose sight of you. And if you find your friend, give of your friendship and it will return to you tenfold. Those who cannot give friendship will rarely receive it and never hold it.

Jean Cocteau

28

Friends find themselves in each
other and thereby gain greater
self-knowledge and self-possession.

J. Glenn Gray

Perfect friendship was created by man himself.
It is the supreme creation.

Jean Cocteau

33

The cultivation of friends and of friendships is certainly of more importance than is generally recognized. If friends are merely recreational resources or convenient distractions from the routine of life, the relationship with them is of minimum value psychologically; it can scarcely be called friendship. The man with no friends has already abandoned himself to the fate of his own self-destructiveness. Psychiatrists realize from clinical experience what poets have proclaimed in inspired verse, that to retreat permanently into the loneliness of one's own soul is to surrender one's claim upon life.

But at best it is hard for human beings to really get together; it is hard for even the best of friends to understand and to feel with one another sufficiently to promote a continuous, peaceful affection. This gives rise to that vague feeling with which we are all familiar of having parted from even our best friend without having fully expressed the affection we feel or fully realized the affection we hope he feels for us.

C.S. Lewis

PLEASE CURE ME!

I really thought I was giving him so much!
And he to me. This giving and receiving seemed
So good: not in terms of what was good for
The two persons we had been, but for the new
Person—us—that was becoming. Even now,
Remembering how I felt then, it seems so right.

But now I've found that we were only strangers
Using each other for our own individual purposes,
No giving or taking—just using, terrible, horrible using!
Can we love only that which is created by our own imagination?
Are we all actually unloving and unlovable?
If this is true, then one is alone, and if one is alone,
Then both lover and beloved are equally unreal
And the dreamer is only as real as his dreams.
It's not that I'm afraid of being hurt again:
Nothing can ever again hurt or heal.
At times I have thought the ectasy is real
Even though those who experience it may have no reality.
For what happened is like a dream in our memory,
A dream in which one is raised by the intensity of loving,
A vibration of delight without desire, for desire is fulfilled
In the joy of loving.
A state not known when awake.
But what, or whom I loved,
Or what in me was loving, I really don't know!
And if it was all meaningless, I want to be cured
Of a desire for something I can't find
And of the shame of never finding it.

Robert Brian

In order to endure, friendship must constantly be remade, renewed, and deepened like life itself.

Ignace Lepp

If little or nothing can be done to make a friendship begin, much has to be done to keep it alive.

Albrecht Goes

40

FRIEND

Our love is real—this I know,
And yet, some people say,
"It's just a shallow love you feel—
It will leave you any day."

I need you so,
But still it's not
The need for me to possess,
But just a need in which a thought
Of you brings happiness.

It's getting Deeper—
This I believe.
And it will grow deeper each day.
But it takes Time and Patience, my friend,
To obtain love, there are things one must pay.

The price of love is sometimes great.
We'll never find it small.
We must give everything we are,
My friend, we must give All.

Your smallest thoughts—
Don't hold them back.
We'll have to learn how to show
Our love for each other, my friend,
In order for it to grow.

Robert Brian

It is not enough for friends to realize that they know and love the same things. This is merely a preliminary phase. In order for friendship to grow and become more fecund it is important to cultivate this embryonic experience. Only progressively, to the degree that their coexistence intensifies and deepens, do friends acquire the unshakable certainty that they are not two solitudes chance has brought together but that the same spiritual sap circulates in them, that anything which might eventually separate them could only be a more or less unfortunate accident. The same light illuminates them; they are en route toward a similar goal even though it may regretably not be by the same path.

Ignace Lepp

44

Life is shared between friends, each living not only his own life but also that of his friends. There must, however, be no question of appropriating the life of another as a master appropriates the life of a slave or as a dictator subjugates the masses under his influence. We make the life of a friend ours with the most total respect for his otherness. This supposes, in the first place, that we let our friend participate in exactly the same way in our life. Friendship, because of the dynamism proper to it, leads us from individual living to a state of shared existence; this implies a veritable metamorphosis of life. Among young people such a metamorphosis is generally effected spontaneously and easily. Sometimes a simple meeting of the eyes, the exchange of a few phrases, a handshake or a small service rendered or received suffice for two people to become conscious of the birth of a mysterious communion between them and open themselves to a mutual osmosis. On the other hand, adults who have known several failures and disappointments in their emotional relationships with others only gradually overcome their mistrust and hesitations and thus become ready for a metamorphosis of their lives through friendship.

Ignace Lepp

45

PART 3

THE VALUE OF FRIENDSHIP

All of us who have experienced friendship have probably discerned a tremendous change in our lives. It is difficult to be totally objective, but friends seem to bring much growth and happiness to each other. Life must be seen, accepted, and challenged. Friends do this to each other. They don't allow for mediocrity or stagnation. The love they share demands that they both constantly seek growth. A person who refuses to change and grow will find it very difficult to be a friend with someone, for the relationship will be too threatening and demanding of him.

Spring is the time of new life, all the buds
    and leaves bloom again,
Life has richer meaning, all the old must fade away.

Everyman must search for the one who'll help him unfold.

    And a friend
is the only one who can free my life and help me
    to be real,
for he brings the life to the bud giving strength as the water of spring.

Everyman must search for the one who'll help him unfold.

    And a friend
is the only one who can understand me for what
    I am,
for he can see the self that is hidden deep, afraid to be shown.

Everyman must search for the one who'll help him unfold.

    And a friend
is the only one who can teach me how to share all
    that I am,
for he creates a new life within that burns and cannot be held.

Everyman must search for the one who'll help him unfold.

    And a friend
is the only one who can free my life and help me to be real.

Kathleen Flynn

It is in and by friendship that we experience ourselves. Through friendship we become aware of our transcendence in relation to the meanness and misery that was our lot when we were a solitary self. Because of friendship we see with different eyes not only our own lives but the entire universe. How marvelous to see again in the company of a friend the landscapes and paintings we had formerly admired alone, to listen with him to symphonies which formerly pleased us! We now see and hear not only with our own eyes and ears but also with those of our friend. Nor is this a question of a simple quantitative addition to the individual capacities of each. The "We" of friendship possesses its own way of seeing and hearing, a capacity of knowing and loving which transcends by far the sum of individual capacities.

Ignace Lepp

For nobody would wish to live without friends,
even if he possessed all other good things.

Aristotle

FRIENDSHIP'S WORTH
by Ignace Lepp

From earliest times innumerable moralists, philosophers, and other thinkers and writers have affirmed that one true friend is worth infinitely more than all the riches and honors of the world. It seems, as a matter of fact, that as long as we have not lived the experience of a solid and deep friendship we can only have a pessimistic vision of human nature. Very often the decisive event in the life of a man is not the accident by which he gained a large fortune or even the success he achieves in athletic, political or intellectual competition, but rather meeting a true friend. However pleasurable be power and wealth, they contribute in a very mediocre fashion to the realization of our vocation as men; they can even become an obstacle to our fulfillment. In any case, they add nothing essential to our solitary self. The spirit of possession almost infallibly engenders avarice in the subject himself and jealousy in others. But it is beyond argument that there can be no adequate fulfillment of the human person without generosity and the forgetting of self. The friend par excellence is he who opens himself to our generosity and lets us share in his. It is, therefore, primarily through this instrumentality that we can exercise ourselves in the practice of generosity and forgetfulness of self. Communication with a friend, that is to say with the intimate life of another, necessarily transcends the domain of having those exchanges of an objective order which are essential to fellowship and even erotic love. It is the direct exchange of one being with another, that is to say veritable communion which friendship demands and encourages.

THE COMFORT OF FRIENDS

They that love beyond the world cannot be separated by it. Death cannot kill what never dies. Nor can spirits ever be divided that love and live in the same divine principle; the root and record of their friendship.

If absence be not death, neither is theirs.

Death is but crossing the world, as friends do the seas; they live in one another still.

For they must need be present, that love and live in that which is Omni-present.

In this divine glass they see face to face; and their converse is free as well as pure.

This is the comfort of friends, that though they may be said to die, yet their friendship and society are, in the best sense, ever present, because immortal.

J. Donald Adams

56

57

The journey we make
between life and death
would be insufferable to me
without the warmth of friendships.

Jean Cocteau

Those who have nothing can share
nothing; those who are going
nowhere can have no fellow-travelers.

C. S. Lewis

Friendship enables us to become simultaneously aware of our riches and our poverty. Since generosity is the condition and the very essence of friendship we must know what we are capable of offering our friend. We are not long in realizing that what we possess is far inferior to what we would like to give our friend. We must, therefore, continue to grow, and it will be in large part because of the generosity of our friend himself that we will be able to increase our riches, both on the level of having and on the level of being.

Friendship is not restricted to encouraging the interior treasures and beauties of friends. It must also encourage their power of action. To exist means to act and create; it is only by acting that man realizes himself, whatever the form of action be. The more he acts, the more he permits the potential of his being to actualize itself. Thought itself is nourished and takes form in action; otherwise, it would be a purely abstract kind of thinking with no hold on reality. Similarly, it is in and through action that we strengthen our capacity for loving. Friendship is capable of considerably increasing man's power of action and creation. In acting with and for each other, friends can accede to a spiritually elevated level of existence which they would not have attempted alone.

Ignace Lepp

60

I have no duty to be anyone's Friend and no man in the world has a duty to be mine. No claims, no shadow of necessity. Friendship is unnecessary, like philosophy, like art, like the universe itself(for God did not need to create). It has no survival value; rather it is one of those things which give value to survival.

C.S. Lewis

62

I LIKE IT!

More—
I need it.
This moment of
real communication
with another person.

I need it—
all my life.
In regular doses.

And how wonderful—
that two people
can make the time and privacy—
often, in the midst
of strangers
rushing by, and noises
grinding in,
to *really*
see
and hear
each other!

Jo Thebaud

PART 4

FRIENDSHIP—IS IT LOVE?

Are friendship and love the same? This is a question many of us have probably asked. The feelings which have surfaced because of friendship are very deep and intense. We want to call our relationship "love" and, indeed, we have told our friends that we "love" them. But some of us still feel uneasy using this word to describe friendship.

Theodor Reik explores this question in the following pages. Perhaps his conclusions are not the same as yours, but his ideas may help to stimulate your own thoughts and ideas.

FRIENDSHIP AND LOVE
by Theodor Reik

The human language, otherwise so discriminating and differentiating, often proves that it has remained a poor medium of expression. Do you love your friend? You feel tempted to answer, "Yes." At the same time you feel that love is not the word to express your emotion adequately. It is certainly not the same feeling a man has for a woman. No, it is not the same, but it is, nevertheless, something similar. You try to distinguish between the two feelings. You say you love her, but you are very fond of your friend. You like him very much, etc. The fact that the object belongs to the other sex makes, of course, a great difference. But is it the only factor? You discuss other matters with the girl you love than you do with your friend, and even if you discuss the same things you do it in a different way, in another spirit. And why is it more difficult to have a friend who belongs to the other sex? Is it that the sexual element disturbs the development of such a relationship? It is certainly untrue that sexual desire differentiates love from friendship. Did we not draw a sharp line between love and sex and did we not point out that one could be distinct from the other? It seems it is difficult to find the differences between love and friendship even between persons of the same sex. For example, a man loves his father, a girl her mother or a teacher, but that does not mean that the object is a friend. And how should we understand a sentence which states that there is more love in friendship than friendship in love? We feel that there are emotional shades and nuances which are hard to grasp.

Whenever you think you understand the differences some similarities or likenesses occur to you. You get confused to such an extent that one moment you think there are sharp distinctions between love and friendship while the next moment you are under the impression that one feeling differs so

slightly from the other that they almost appear identical. You assume then, that a great many of the difficulties you meet are rooted in the inadequacy of our language. They are of a verbal kind. Nevertheless, in addition to this factor there are certain delicate points differentiating the two emotions which originate from their psychical nature.

Should we start with the impression that friendship is not as *intense* as love? Immediately we shall see many instances in which friendship between men, for example, proved to be stronger than the affection for a woman or in which the friendship outlasted the love-relationship. When we point out that friendship usually does not plunge us into trouble and misery as love does we shall see illustrations in which a friendship was the undoing of many people. Nevertheless it is our definite impression that friendship does not have the same urgency and insistency, the same violence as love. You might miss a friend and long for him but the emotional

temperature of this feeling is different from the painful nostalgia with which love sometimes fills us.

Could you speak of "passionate friendship"? It sounds a bit gaunt, exaggerated or ridiculous. It even sounds somewhat odd when we hear a man say he loves a friend. Nowadays we feel that this is an exaggeration. We are aware that the language of friendship has changed during the centuries. Comparing the manifestations of friendship today with the expressions of the past, we cannot fail to recognize that the language of friendship has become less ardent. It has lost the expression of enthusiasm, of gushing. In the time of Shakespeare you could unhesitatingly have declared that you loved a friend passionately. Today the adjective does not go well with the noun. Even an essay like Emerson's on friendship speaks about the subject in an exuberant way, which means that it sounds this way to our ears, while it did not sound like that to the contemporaries of Emerson. Reading novels of a hundred years ago we are aware that people talked about their friendship in a way which would fill us with embarrassment today. We do not gush about this emotion any more. We prefer not to discuss it at all. We do not like protestations of friendship which have a passionate character. Listening to the talk of men about the emotions which surround their friendships in the language of Emerson would sound to us as if a musical passage which should be played piano is performed fortissimo. Friendship today is thrifty in its verbal expressions. Does that mean that there are no longer any intimate friendships as in the past, that relationships like David's and Jonathan's, Orestes' and Pylades', are unthinkable? Certainly not, just as in our day we often hear of proof of true friendships, not only on the battlefield but also under the hardships of civilian life. Nevertheless, our final impression is that friendship also differs from love in degree. It does not have the same passionate atmosphere. It is cooler.

There is nothing of the ardent zeal here which so often appears in love. Nothing of the self-forgetfulness, the full surrender, the superabundance of emotions. Friendship is sounder and saner. It can never be compared with being drunk and its moods cannot be called insanity or madness. Friendship does not hit you like a cataclysm or an earthquake. Friends in one another's company might feel very pleased

with each other but they are not wildly happy, enchanted or delirious as lovers sometimes are. Friendship is a warming open fireplace while love is a house on fire.

If your impression is correct it would mean that there is a difference of intensity or degree in the two emotions. This finally results in qualitative differences. I have already mentioned the contrast between our feelings when we miss a love-object, or a friend. Friendship does not develop those permanent, strong desires which lovers feel when their loved one is absent. Friends need not stick together to belong together.

It appears further that the feature of idealization so characteristic of those in love is unnecessary for friendship. You appreciate the excellent qualities of your friend but you also know his shortcomings and faults. Friendship need not be blind as love usually is. It can be critical and yet tolerant, which love very seldom is. Your friend does not represent your ego-ideal as the beloved does. At best he is part of your ego-model. We said love begins with the wish, "I would like to be you," or the desire to change one's personality with that of the beloved person. Nothing of such a possessive character can be observed in friendship. Apparently it is not our wish to be like our friend but rather a wish to have some of his qualities which we lack. Do you really want to be your friend, or even be like your friend? Isn't it rather a desire on your part to have some of his traits or endowments? You wish to be him or to be like him only in a certain direction, but you would not care to possess all of his characteristics and are quite satisfied to be yourself. The stoic philosopher Zeno when asked, "What is a friend?" answered, "Another I." The answer is much more appropriate for the love-object whereas a friend is only a certain and definite part of "another I." Our thesis that love can be traced back to unconscious envy, jealousy and greed toward the object concerned the whole person. The object is wanted to the very last morsel. In the case of friendship, only certain intellectual, emotional, mental or physical qualities of the person appear desirable. Our unconscious envy concerns only those and not all of his person and nature.

Here is another and, it seems to me, very important difference. You feel, when in love, that your object is superior to you. For the man the beloved is, so to speak, a higher being, an angel. Such an inferiority feeling, such humbleness toward the object, is certainly lacking in friendship. You might recognize and acknowledge your friend's superiority in one direction or another but you do not think that he is your superior in every way. Not only is such an attitude lacking in friendship—it would make friendship impossible. It seems that friendship can only flourish on the level of equality. A pronounced and conscious superiority or inferiority of one's self or of the object is a serious handicap in the development of true friendship. Goethe called Eckermann his friend but Eckermann would not have dared to call himself a friend of Goethe. He was too aware of the other's superiority. A person who is so much superior to you might be very friendly but he is not your friend. To be so called by him is certainly something to be proud of, but such a distinction cannot be used in treating him as a friend. It is one-sided. It will awaken feelings of pride and will favor love, respect and admiration, but not friendship. You cannot be the friend of a genius when you feel only a bit better than mediocre yourself. The feeling of equal value is a necessary condition to mature friendship. If the superiority of the friend is emphasized, mutual friendship becomes impossible. The human distance is too great to be bridged.

Let us now compare love and friendship in another direction. You are in love with a girl. Does that exclude being in love with another girl at the same time? It

certainly does, if you are not too neurotic. Romeo's passion for Rosalind vanishes immediately when he sees Juliet. There is no place for another woman as Tristan feels his fateful love for Isolde. Love means singleness of the object. It demands like the God of the Old Testament, "You shall have no other God besides me." Is the same exclusiveness valid for friendship? No. Friendship, it is true, is no mass article. One who is everyone's friend is nobody's friend, but you can have several friends, and good ones too, at the same time. The difference which the two emotions present in this direction is caused by the different claims they make. Love is much more pretentious, its demands are greater. It engulfs the victim like a maelstrom. Friendship carries you like a friendly river. Love takes possession of your whole heart while friendship claims only a part of you. It is not as consuming a passion, does not engross you and does not tax you to the utmost. It does not make excessive demands;

it has a more democratic character. It does not want to own you; it merely wants a place in your life.

Are these differences which were for the most part neglected in the psychological analysis of love and friendship clarified sufficiently to attempt a solution of our problem? Is the insight which we gained from these impressions sufficient to venture a guess about the essential difference? Love is a reaction-formation to envy, jealousy and greed. Friendship is a reaction to original feelings of rivalry and competition which were aroused by the unconscious acknowledgment of certain qualities of the object. Some of your friend's traits or characteristics appear to be attractive to the degree that you would like to have them for yourself. He is a supplement of yourself but only in a certain way. Some features of his character or nature are enviable. The original feeling which the observation of his presence or his actions awakens in you is a wish to overcome him, to conquer him in this or that direction. He arouses feelings of competitiveness in you. You want to measure yourself with him and to be the better of the two. The emotional reaction then sets in. These original impulses are rejected, the tendency to fight and to overcome him changes into the wish to help him, to unite your own efforts with his, to join him and to combine your energies. The reaction which follows the initial tendency to fight sweeps the original impulses away and gives in to the opposite strivings. Rivalry and competitiveness disappear from the emotional surface. They retreat into the unconscious where they are kept alive, ready to break through when friendship dissolves. The earlier tendencies lurk around the corner which in some cases is easily turned. The unconscious effect of envy and jealousy in friendship cannot be denied but it is not as concentrated as it is in love.

The ingredients of friendship are slightly different since its unconscious roots reveal merely a stimulus to rivalry and not so much to envy and jealousy, as explained by its less passionate character. The fact that it becomes possible only when two friends are about equal in their achievements and like traits discriminates the relationship from love.

In the realm of friendship the unconscious contest leads also to a point where it threatens to become hostile. If the reaction then proves less intense it is because the tension which preceded the formation of friendship was not as strong as the one which preceded love. Before the forming of friendship there is hostility in the air too, but of a less fateful character, more like that prior to a wrestling match than to a duel. Not who will survive but who will be victorious should be decided. In the case of love the opponents make up their minds, so to speak, at the last moment not to fight to the death but to embrace and kiss. The future friends also raise their arms for the blow

but instead of tussling they shake hands and walk off together to have a drink. What unconsciously prepared the ground for friendship does not concern the whole personality. It is not a decision on which life and death depend. The tide never turns as high as it does just before love sets in. If it did, worship or love would be the result of the following reaction, not friendship. In love the end is really a giving up of one's own personality, the melting of two human beings. This does not take place in friendship.

In fully developed friendship the results of the emotional reaction appear on the surface; kindness in the place of hostility, the tendency to spare the friend, to support him instead of the impulse to harm him, a successful effort to help him reach his aims instead of a desire to frustrate him.

Are there no traces left of the old and now unconscious spirit of contest and competition? Of course. You are very ready to praise your friend but you are not so happy when others praise him—quite in contrast to the attitude of a lover. The original contest continues to exist also in the form of peaceful emulation between friends. It even permeates the Christian friendship of brotherhood in which everyone competes with another for the love of Christ, and in which friends incite each other in God's work. The highest form of friendship is reached when competition is replaced by the gentler form of emulation. Even the concealed activity of hostility is somewhere kept alive. You seldom overlook a mistake your friend has made. Is your friend a well-wisher? Certainly, as far as his conscious thoughts reach, but four hundred years before psychoanalysis discovered the existence of the ambivalence of feelings between the most intimate of friends La Rochefoucauld remarked that there is something in the calamity of our friends which does not displease us.

PART 5

THE EXPERIENCE OF FRIENDSHIP

It is impossible for anyone to explain the experience of friendship without giving concrete examples of it. Because of its nature, no one person's experience is ever going to be the same as another's. Even the shared experience of two friends is different to a degree for each of them.

Friends usually experience a joy in sharing; sharing one's feelings, one's ideas and ideals, hurts, dreams, and fears. It involves common experiences such as late night discussions, painful confrontations, swimming together, double-dating, and walks.

The total experience which is friendship consists of many mini-experiences which become a relationship. Because all of us and our friends have such divergent mini-experiences, our total experience of friendship is understandably going to be different from that of others.

The wind was blowing hard that day,
Kind of chilly—but warm for December.
There were many things I wanted to say,
But they were unnecessary—if you remember.

The cliffs were high, you sat on the edge
It scared me—so close to death's grip.
For a while I sat with you there on the ledge,
So afraid that you might slip.

We climbed all over those cliffs that day,
Every moment was filled with love,
Just laughing, enjoying everything along the way,
And stopping to gaze at the blue sky above.

It was over too soon, the sun was getting low.
We had to start back home again.
Neither of us really wanted to go,
I guess no one wants to part with a friend.

Robert Brian

Bit by bit, nevertheless, it comes over us that we shall never again hear the laughter of our friend, that this one garden is forever locked against us. And at that moment begins our true mourning, which, though it may not be rending, is yet a little bitter. For nothing, in truth, can replace that companion. Old friends cannot be created out of hand. Nothing can match the treasure of common memories, of trials endured together, of quarrels and reconciliations and generous emotions.

Antoine de Saint Exupery

82

There's so much
yet so little
to say.

My mother's people had a way
of separating friends.
They used a ditch that gradually widened.
Those to be parted walked along,
hand in hand,
on opposite sides
until they could no longer touch.

And what did they feel
as each inch became
an earth between them?
What do you and I now feel?
They thought of precious yesterdays,
of empty tomorrows,
of treasured joys and childish dreams.
As their eyes met this one last time,
unwanted tears said more than any words.
And when they turned to walk

their separate ways,
they knew as we know
that something immutable had died
that something fleeting had become eternal,
that much had been earned
and too much lost.

"For to part is to die a little."

L. D. Streiker

86

When one has been greatly isolated and restricted in movement, one deeply feels the value of openness, of freedom and expansiveness. Life takes on an exquisite meaning, an exhilarating richness. When one has lived in total darkness, one piercingly appreciates the sunlight, the fireside, the beacon, the beginning dawn. When one is cut off from human companionship, one discovers a deep reverence for friendship, for the one who stands by in the hour of need and shame.

Clark E. Moustakas

87

FRIENDSHIP

And a youth said, Speak to us of Friendship. And he answered, saying: Your friend is your needs answered. He is your field which you sow with love and reap with thanksgiving. And he is your board and your fireside. For you come to him with your hunger, and you seek him for peace.

When your friend speaks his mind you fear not the "nay" in your own mind, nor do you withhold the "ay." And when he is silent your heart ceases not to listen to his heart; For without words, in friendship, all thoughts, all desires, all expectations are born and shared, with joy that is unacclaimed. When you part from your friend, you grieve not; For that which you love most in him may be clearer in his absence, as the mountain to the climber is clearer from the plain.

And let there be no purpose in friendship save the deepening of the spirit. For love that seeks aught but the disclosure of its own mystery is not love but a net cast forth: and only the unprofitable is caught.

And let your best be for your friend. If he must know the ebb of your tide, let him know its flood also. For what is your friend that you should seek him with hours to kill? Seek him always with hours to live. For it is his to fill your need, but not your emptiness. And in the sweetness of friendship let there be laughter, and sharing of pleasures. For in the dew of little things the heart finds its morning and is refreshed.

Kahlil Gibran

YOUR NAME

After all these years
your very name
sends the inward sinews
straining after wasted dreams.
And on my cheek
I feel a single tear turn cold.

Within the archives of forgotten hopes
I put your name away
until it seeks me out again
or fades like all desires.

L. D. Streiker

A walk in the valley.
I came in from the night.
I was lonely.
Your light was on,
You were there.
    Thanks.

A Friend